Fun & Facts

First published
in the UK 1996
by Sapling, an imprint
of Boxtree Limited
Broadwall House, 21 Broadwall,
London SE1 9PL.

First published in the USA in 1996 by
Price Stern Sloan, Inc, a member of
The Putnam & Grosset Group, New
York, New York, USA

Copyright © 1996 by MCA
Publishing Rights, a Division of
MCA, Inc. All rights reserved.
Flipper is TM and © 1996 by
Universal Studios, Inc.
All rights reserved.
Published by arrangement with
MCA Publishing Rights, a Division
of MCA, Inc.

10 9 8 7 6 5 4 3 2 1

ISBN: 0 7522 2251 1

This publication may not be
reproduced, transmitted or held in a
retrieval system in part or in whole
in any form or using any electronic,
mechanical, photocopying or
recording process or any other
process without the publisher
having first given permission in
writing.

Except in the United States of
America this book is sold subject to
the condition that it shall not, by way
of trade or otherwise, be lent,
resold, hired out or otherwise
circulated without the publisher's
prior consent in any form of binding
or cover other than that in which it is
published and without a similar
condition being imposed upon a
subsequent purchaser.

Printed and bound by Dai Nippon (HK)
Printing Ltd, Hong Kong

A catalogue record for this book is
available from the British Library

Based on a motion picture screenplay by Arthur Weiss and story by Ricou Browning and Jack Cowden.

Written by
David Max

Illustrated by
Andrea Tachiera

Book Designed by
Leslie Fitch

Based on the Motion Picture Screenplay Written by Alan Shapiro

Facts About Dolphin Bodies

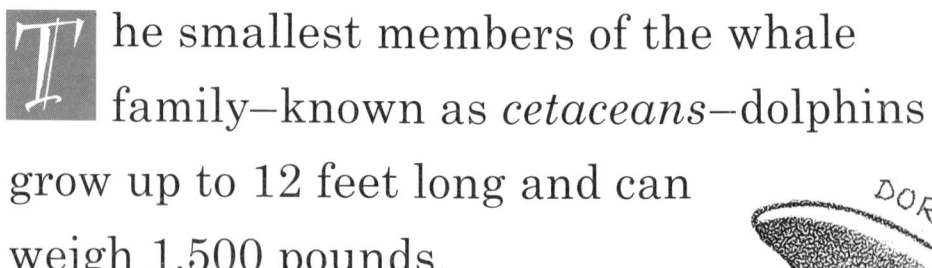

The smallest members of the whale family—known as *cetaceans*—dolphins grow up to 12 feet long and can weigh 1,500 pounds.

Did you know that dolphins have bellybuttons just like people? That's because they're mammals—not fish. Not only do they have lungs and need to breathe air, they're warm-blooded. Their babies are born alive and they drink their mother's milk.

Flipper says:
Dolphins are really fantastic—if I do say so myself! In the movie about me, Sandy found that out right away! You see, we fit into our environment by putting together the best parts of mammals and the best parts of fish! Talk about **SMART!**

Facts About Dolphin Bodies 3

A dolphin's nose is on top of its head! It's called a blowhole. Dolphins close their blowholes when they dive. They don't breathe automatically, either. They have to think about it!

BLOWHOLE

Trees and dolphins have something in common. Their round, pointed teeth have rings— just like a tree does—one for each year they have lived. The best way to tell the age of a dolphin is by counting the rings on its teeth!

EYE

PECTORAL FIN

Dolphin eyes are protected from the stinging saltwater by a clear, jelly-like layer that looks like tears. They can swivel their eyes to see forward or to either side of their face.

A strong sense of smell is not high on a dolphin's priority list. Maybe it's because they eat raw fish! A few years ago, some dolphins were being moved from one animal park to another. When they were driven through a cloud of mosquito spray, they started squawking wildly. We don't know whether they squawked because the spray smelled bad or because it made their sensitive skin sting.

Different Kinds of Dolphins

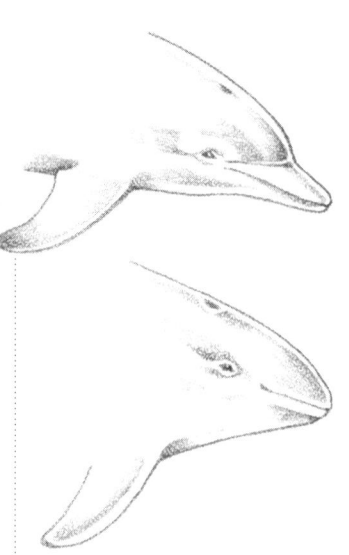

The easiest way to tell the difference between a dolphin and a porpoise is the shape of the head. Porpoises have smaller heads and shorter snouts.

There are 25 different kinds of saltwater dolphins and 5 kinds of freshwater dolphins. Freshwater dolphins are only found in a few large rivers in India, Asia, and South America.

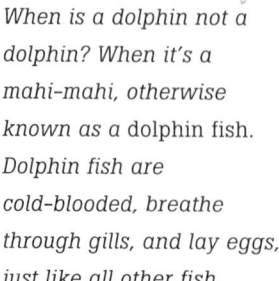

When is a dolphin not a dolphin? When it's a mahi-mahi, otherwise known as a dolphin fish. Dolphin fish are cold-blooded, breathe through gills, and lay eggs, just like all other fish.

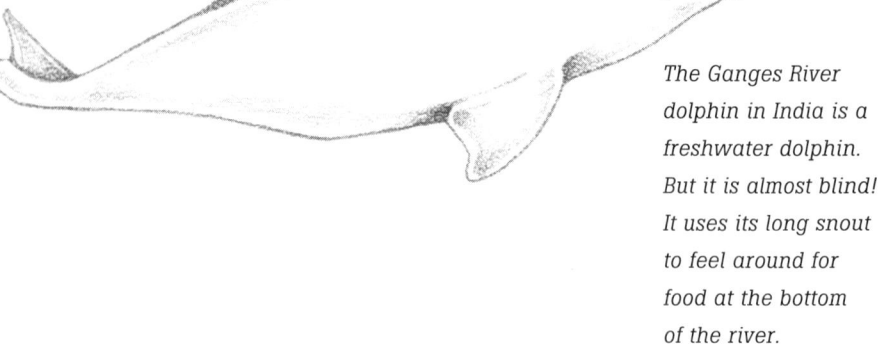

The Ganges River dolphin in India is a freshwater dolphin. But it is almost blind! It uses its long snout to feel around for food at the bottom of the river.

Different Kinds of Dolphins 5

Flipper says:
I just know I'm a Florida dolphin because they're the best! All dolphins are smart, of course, but we just happen to be underwater geniuses!

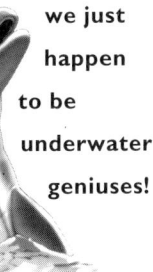

Of all the different dolphin groups that live in the world's oceans, the Florida bottlenose dolphin is the smartest. All other groups of dolphins are still cetaceans, but the Florida dolphins are used in sea parks and experimental studies all over the world because they learn tricks the fastest.

45 million years ago, the ancestors of dolphins looked like wolves and lived on land at the edges of the sea. If you compare the skeletons of modern dolphins with those of their ancestors, you can see how, over time, their front legs became flippers. Over the ages, their back legs turned into tiny bones behind their ribs.

Would you believe that dolphins have hairy noses? Newborn baby dolphins are born with a few hairs on their snouts that are leftovers from their wolf-like ancestors.

The bones in dolphin flippers are a lot like the bones in a human hand. The skin around their fingers grew together to make paddles for swimming.

Dolphin Family Life

Dolphins live in families, or *pods*. Harbor dolphins cruise the coastal waters in pods of 2 to 5. Bottlenose dolphin families have about 5 to 10 members, and deep-sea dolphin pods can have as many as 100,000 members!

Since they have to start breathing air right away, dolphin babies are born tail first. Tipping the scale at 30 pounds and 3½ feet long when they are born, they swim right to the surface. If they need help, dolphin mothers push their babies up and hold them while they get used to surfacing for air.

Dolphin pods usually have a leader and there are rules that everyone has to obey—just like in human families!

Flipper says:
I'm glad I found my dolphin family again. They sure came in handy when I needed them to help protect me and Sandy. Besides, at least we dolphins can speak the same language —if you know what I mean!

Babies travel with their mothers for up to 3 years. Female dolphins are grown up at 6 years of age, and male dolphins at 12 years old.

Dolphin Family Life

Baby dolphins can keep up with their mothers, no matter how fast they swim. They are carried along by the force of the water moving past the mother's body. Swimming in this envelope of moving water is called *echelon swimming*.

Dolphin milk is squirted into the baby's mouth through the mother's nipple. Babies begin to eat a few fish by the time they are 6 months old, but often keep nursing for a year. Mother dolphins bite the fish heads off so dolphin babies won't have trouble chewing and swallowing.

If a baby wanders too far away from her, the mother dolphin may hold the baby tightly between her flippers.

Ways Dolphins Help One Another

Flipper says:
We always help one another out. Remember when my pod helped me get rid of that hammerhead shark named Scar? He was about to eat Sandy! I might not have been able to fight Scar off alone.

When babies are born, female dolphins called *aunties* sometimes help the mother. The aunties also baby-sit for the little dolphins. Sometimes mother dolphins and aunties will circle the babies, making a safe playpen for them to swim in freely.

One sea park dolphin gave birth right before a show started. The other dolphins were so excited, they all—including a large pilot whale—refused to perform because they wanted to keep checking on the new baby!

Dolphins swim in formation. A *navigating formation* looks like a wedge, with the babies in the center for protection. A *parade formation* looks like a circle, and is used for swimming in the open ocean. The whole pod can then keep an eye out for danger and attack any enemies. In a hunting formation, dolphins break into small groups to herd fish together.

When a member of the pod is sick or hurt, the dolphins will swim on either side of the sick one, supporting it with their flippers. They carry it up to the surface so it can breathe. Others bring food.

With only two or three favorite spots along their home coastlines, individual dolphin pods always end up coming back to these spots again and again. That way they get to know their neighbors—both human and non-human—very well.

Although some fishermen think dolphins feed on the same schools of fish the fishermen catch to make their money, dolphins actually prefer the kinds of fish known as *trash*. That means people won't eat the same fish that dolphins like best.

Flipper says: I like to have lots of different kinds of friends. Dolphins are the coolest, but birds and seals always know what's happening topside. For example, remember when I gave Pelican Pete some fish? Well, he gave me some important news in return. It always pays to be well-informed!

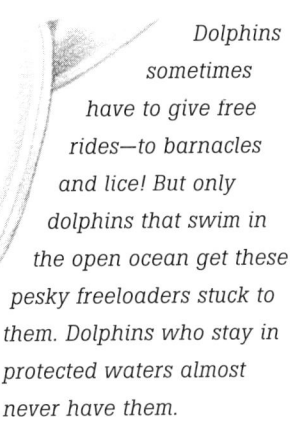

Dolphins share their favorite spots with many different fish, birds, and mammals, such as seals, manatees or sea cows, sharks, whales, tuna, pelicans, seagulls, and even humans. Some are enemies, some are friends, some are both— and some are lunch!

Dolphins sometimes have to give free rides—to barnacles and lice! But only dolphins that swim in the open ocean get these pesky freeloaders stuck to them. Dolphins who stay in protected waters almost never have them.

How Dolphins Talk and Hear

The language of dolphins sounds like this: Chirp! Whistle! Beep! Creak! Groan! Bark! Click, click, click! *They also clap their jaws, smack their flukes on the water, whine, and even make a sound like laughing. In addition, dolphins make some sounds that people can't hear.*

There are two separate sides to a dolphin's blowhole, both with muscles that act like lips. Dolphins can use the two sides to make two separate sets of sounds at the same time—both clicks and whistles. This would be the same as a person whispering while having a different conversation out loud—and both at the same time!

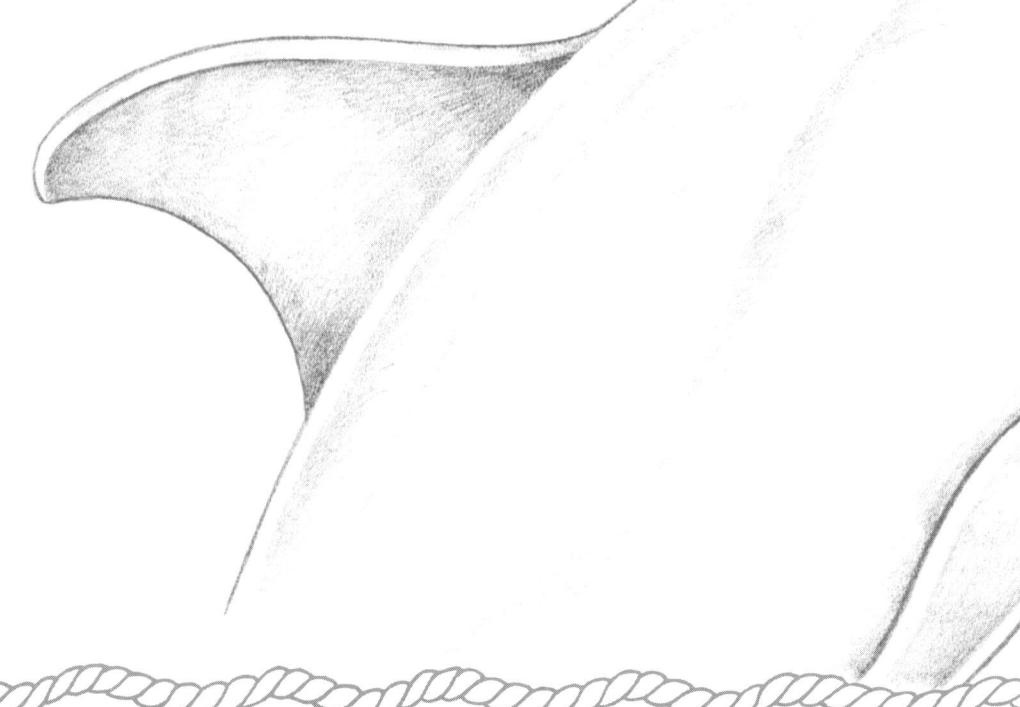

Flipper says:
When I first met Sandy, I thought he could speak dolphin. How was I supposed to know it was a game machine making that beep noise? But even though he couldn't speak any useful language at the time, he was definitely a quick learner! Bright boy, that one!

How Dolphins Talk and Hear

Dolphins can imitate lots of sounds: fish, ducks, seagulls, boat engines, and even human language. Some dolphins have been taught how to count in English, and even say a few words and simple sentences. The dolphins weren't just mimicking, the way parrots do, either. They were actually using the words correctly!

Different sounds mean different things in dolphin language. When frightened, they make a noise that sounds like Whistle-squawk! *A long series of very loud fast whistles means, "I'm lonely." Jaw clacks are usually made to scare another dolphin. Tail slaps on the water mean, "I'm mad!" A long series of clicks means that food is nearby.*

Each dolphin has its own personal whistle that all other dolphins recognize. Blindfolded dolphins can pick out the whistle sounds of all the other dolphins they know—every single time!

Is it possible to hear better through your jaw bone than through your ears? It is for dolphins! They have ear openings just behind their eyes. But they're so tiny they don't work that well. Dolphins hear mainly through their jaws.

How Dolphins Talk and Hear

Dolphins always let humans and other dolphins know when they don't like something. They open and close their mouths, bob their heads up and down in a "go away" motion, or make a *Whah-whah* sound to say, "Cut that out before I get really mad!"

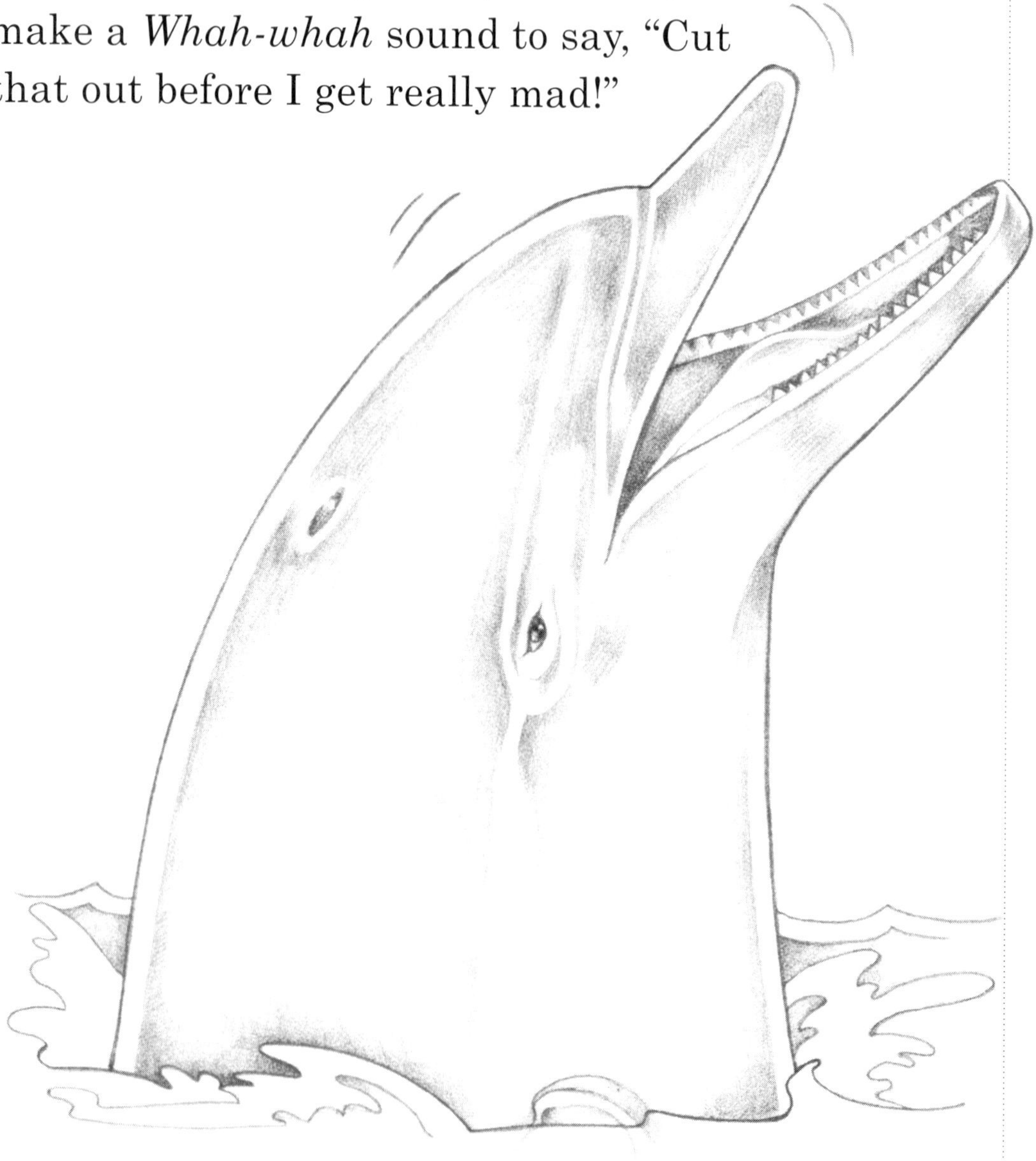

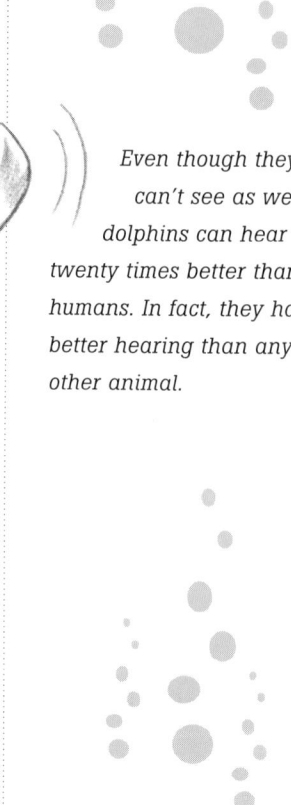

Even though they can't see as well, dolphins can hear twenty times better than humans. In fact, they have better hearing than any other animal.

How Dolphins Talk and Hear   13

Singing acts are very popular at sea parks. But dolphins aren't good singers the way some cetaceans, like humpback whales, are. Dolphins can be trained to "sing" by getting yummy rewards for certain groups of whistles and squawks. When a dolphin in the wild makes those sounds, however, it means they're very grouchy or upset.

Swimming really fast with lots of splashing is one way dolphins use their bodies to talk. That lets nearby dolphins know something weird is happening. Sometimes a dolphin will turn and stare at the others. This can let them know it doesn't like what they're doing.

Maybe people need a good night's sleep, but dolphins don't. They just take short naps. When they wake up and start making sounds again, they sound sleepy—just like people do.

A mother dolphin will playfully nip her baby to show affection. But when she nips harder, it is to show the baby it's being way too naughty.

Dolphin Sonar

Flipper says:
I can find anything with my sonar! You want a used watch? Or a quarter? Or a big can full of evil smelly stuff? I can handle it! But wouldn't you rather have a delicious mullet instead?

Like bats, dolphins use sound waves to "see." This is called *echolocation*. Sound travels 5 times faster underwater, and dolphins use it to find food.

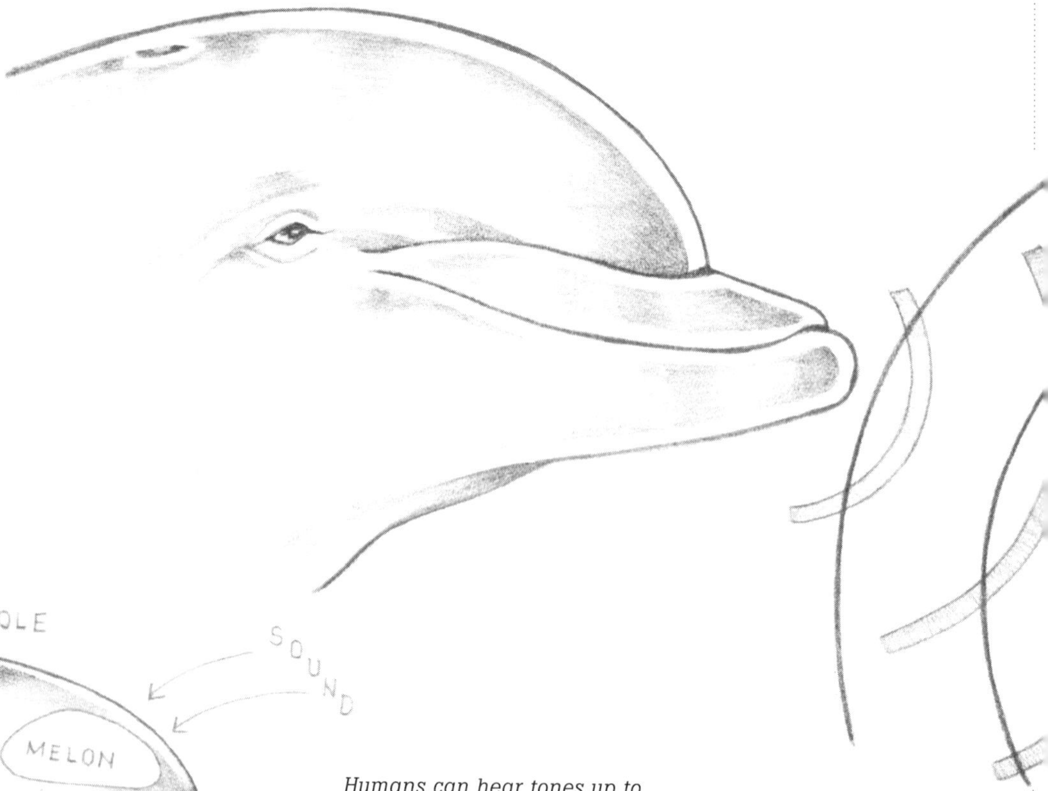

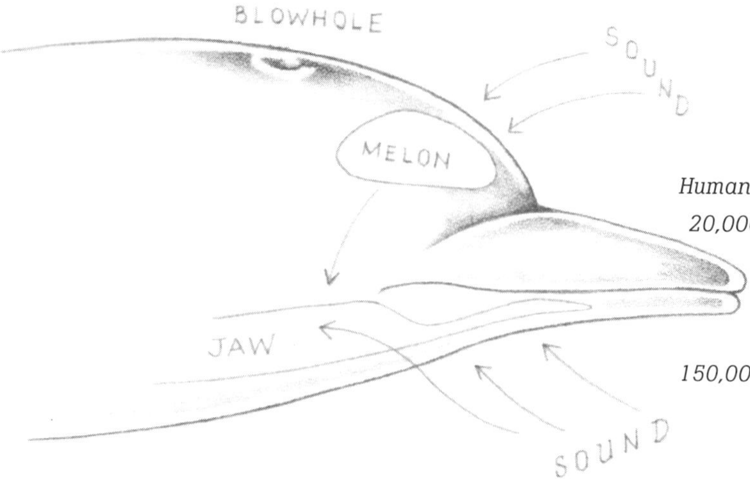

BLOWHOLE
SOUND
MELON
JAW
SOUND

Humans can hear tones up to 20,000 cycles per second. But dolphins can "hear" sound echoes with tones up to 150,000 cycles per second!

Dolphin Sonar

olphins can send 2,000 clicks per second. Their brains can figure out what all those click echoes mean in just one second. This makes them sensitive enough to find a fish the size of a tiny minnow from 10 feet away. One blindfolded dolphin found half a vitamin at the bottom of its tank!

The reason echolocation is used to describe dolphin sonar is because each dolphin click bounces off objects in the water, creating an echo. The dolphin "reads" the echo of those clicks and can tell what the object is, how far away, how big it is, what direction it's going in, and how fast it's going.

People figured out that dolphins used sonar because dolphins were able to avoid swimming into capture nets—even in murky water. They turned away before even touching the nets!

Dolphin sonar clicks are formed in air sacs located near a hollow in its skull, right by its blowhole. This hollow is called the melon. The echoes that bounce back are picked up by the dolphin's chin. The vibration then travels back through the jawbone to the inner ear.

Sonar helps dolphins "see" when they're out of the water, too. A blindfolded dolphin can jump a barrier that is above water just by using its sonar.

Flipper says:
I figured out early that doing tricks gets you a great snack. Remember the time I snatched Sandy's tuna sub right out of his hand? He liked that trick! I liked that snack! Besides, we're buddies. I teach him tricks, and he teaches me tricks—

but mine are better!

Playing is one of the ways people find out about intelligence. Since dolphins like to play more than any other animal, they are definitely very smart!

Boats make great toys, and *bow riding* is one of the dolphins' favorite games. Dolphins also like to leap and surf with the waves created as a ship moves through the water.

This is my photo album from the movie they made about me! Of course a dolphin can have a photo album—if there's a dry place to keep it! This is Uncle Porter and that's his fishing boat. It's messy but great!

Here are my best friends from the movie: Sandy looking grouchy, Porter and his girlfriend, Cathy, and Sandy when he first got to the island.

Isn't Porter weird?

Oh, and here's Sandy and Kim sitting on Porter's dock.

This was the best tasting part of the movie! Kids threw in a quarter, then I brought back a penny! Sandy made lots of money, and I got lots of fish! Porter took the money, but I got to keep the fish!

Hah!

Here's me eating again!

And here's Marvin, the genius kid who wouldn't talk until he got a little help from me! Takes one to know one!

This is Pete the Pelican. He likes eating, too! Here's a close-up of our little business.

Love that sign!

Me, eating again, of course. Kim told Sandy it takes a lot of food to make me happy!

Sandy is a smart boy.
He did just what I told him to!

After I taught Marvin to talk and swim, everyone got lunch but me!

Here are the two bad guys in the movie: Dirk "The Jerk" Moran (who shoots dolphins) and Scar, the hammerhead shark (who eats dolphins).

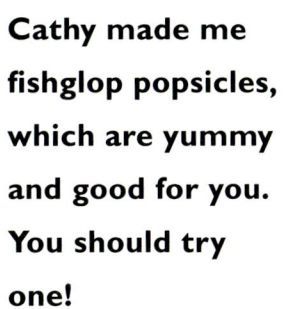

Cathy made me fishglop popsicles, which are yummy and good for you. You should try one!

Dirk and Scar couldn't get rid of me!

It's a good thing I was cured because I had to save Sandy from getting killed by Dirk. I knocked him right off his boat into the water.

Even Cathy, who hates fighting, liked that a lot!

He climbed out, but Porter socked him in the nose and knocked him right back in! Hah!

Here's me playing ball and Porter laughing while Dirk gets arrested for dumping poison in the water, hurting kids and dolphins, and generally being an all-around idiot!

This was the scary part when I got really sick from the poison Dirk dumped.

But Cathy and everyone knew just what to do to make me better.

This is when Sandy says goodbye to Cathy.

Porter and Cathy got engaged—about time!

Here's Kim giving me a pat on the back!

Yippee!
They don't call
me Flipper
for nothing!

Dolphin Tricks 17

A toy can be anything! Dolphins will play with leaves, feathers, seaweed, pieces of floating wood, balls, the fish they're eating—even boats and people!

Young dolphins like to tease each other by holding a fish out to a friend, then snatching it back just before it's taken!

Dolphins like to play so much they often play games with other sea animals. They especially like to harass sea turtles by bumping into them and dragging them around.

Of course, dolphins can learn to play human games, but they also make up their own games which they will teach humans to play. One of their favorite games is "catch." *They try to get people to play with them by tossing whatever they can find at them!*

Some dolphins will swim up small tidal creeks, then beach themselves and play at mud sliding. Dolphins just wanna have fun!

Water is a great toy, too—and there's plenty of that where dolphins live! They bodysurf in the waves, do somersaults, leaps, jumps, flips, and tail-walks.

What Dolphins Eat and How They Catch It

How does a dolphin get a fast-food dinner? By following fishing boats and eating the trash fish that get thrown back overboard! They also follow shrimp boats and eat the small bottom fish that get kicked up by the drag nets.

Flipper says:
I eat 15 pounds of fish a day—and that's a lot of fishing! It helps when you can get team effort going. That's why I trained Kim and Sandy to bring me fish. But I can catch fish on my own, too! I like smacking them out of the water—just the way I smacked mean old Dirk off the boat! Smooth move, huh?

Nobody likes piggy eaters, and that includes dolphins! They usually swallow their fish whole, but sometimes they'll bite the head neatly off the fish that have sharp spines or dorsal fins. Dolphins always turn the fish around so it goes down head first. Scales can catch in their throat and cause unsightly dinner accidents!

Fish are, of course, the usual favorites for a dolphin's main meal, but sometimes dolphins like a nice pre-meal appetizer of shrimp. Dolphins get shrimp by poking them up from the bottom of the ocean with their snouts.

Appetizers don't always have to be that fancy. Dolphins will eat anything, including hermit crabs and worms!

What Dolphins Eat and How They Catch It

Garbage boats attract all kinds of things—including some of the fish dolphins like to eat. Following garbage boats is another easy way to get dinner.

Dolphins use sonar to catch their food, too. Bouncing a sound wave off the fish helps them "see" it.

Even without hands dolphins have invented tools! The ones who live near coral reefs use the reef to corner the fish. Then they race in to grab it!

Some dolphins like to smack fish out of the water with their tails. When the fish hits the water, it is too stunned to swim away. That's when the dolphin gobbles it down!

After finding a school of fish, dolphins work together by forming a circle until the school is in a tight group. One by one, each dolphin goes in the circle to feed.

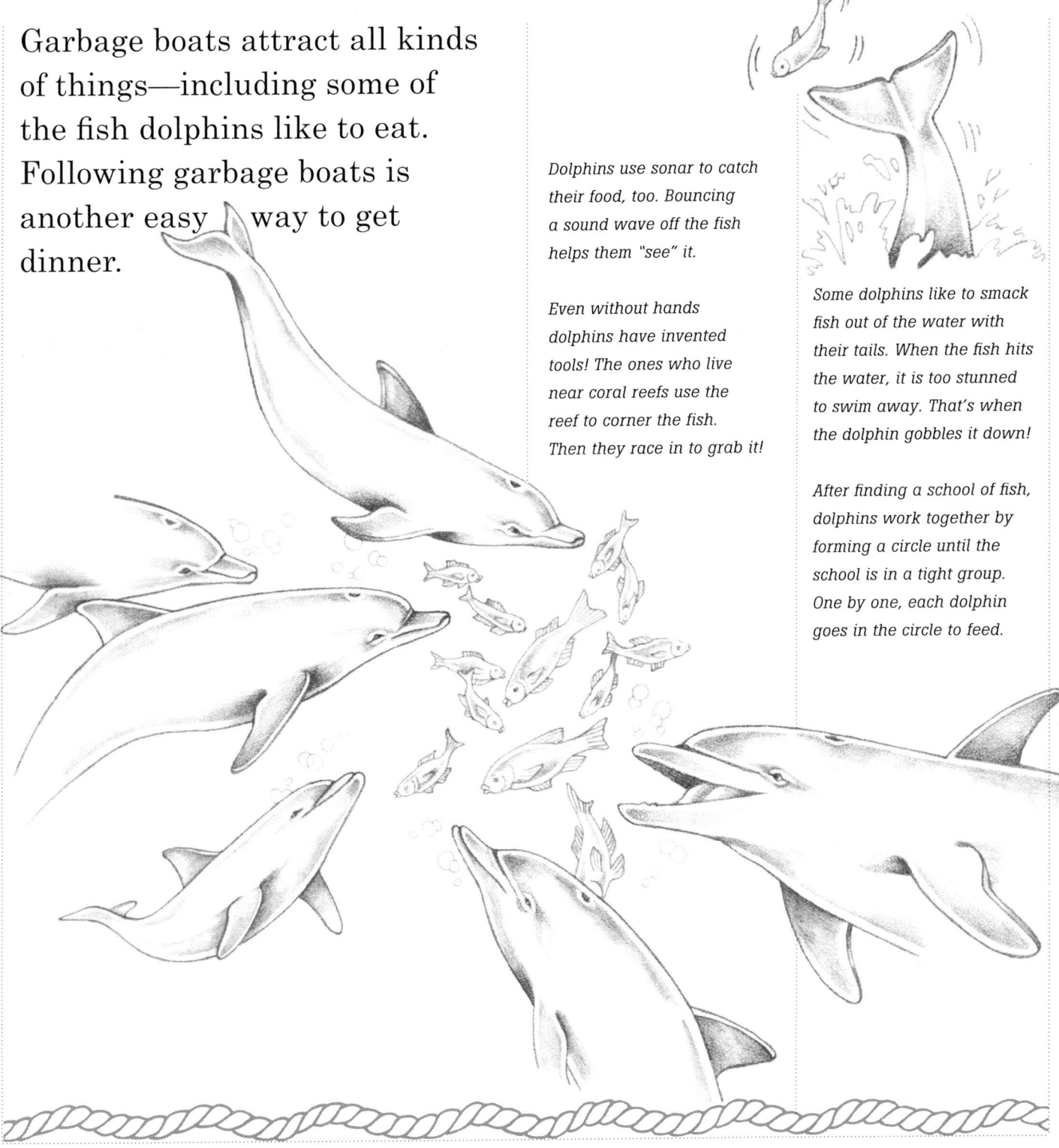

A while ago, the U.S. Navy developed and built an underwater laboratory to study creatures of the sea and their environment. Dolphins from the Navy Sealab programs were trained to dive down 1,000 feet, but only if they were given lots of yummy rewards! Usually dolphins will only dive about 100 feet.

Dolphins can hold their breath for up to 7 minutes on a dive. That means they don't need to decompress to get the nitrogen out of their systems the way deep-diving human scuba divers must before they surface. It also means they can dive over and over again. This makes dolphins very useful for helping humans in the sea.

When dolphins bow ride, they can go as fast as the ship is going. But this is because they are getting help from the force of the moving wave. As long as they position themselves just right in the wave, they can keep up with the fastest boat!

Dolphin Super Swimmers

Can people learn from dolphins? You bet! The different ways dolphins use their smooth skin, their special shape, and the speed of the waves to go fast, may help humans design better and faster boats.

When swimming at the surface, 1 or 2 times a minute is the normal dolphin breathing rate. But when swimming fast, this rate may increase to 5 or 6 times a minute.

Flipper says:
I'm pretty fast! Remember how I kept up with Sandy when I was swimming and he was riding his bike? But I decided to let him win. I also know a good speed trick or two—like the time I kept up with Porter's trawler when they went out into the ocean.

Some people think that dolphins can swim as fast as 50 mph. But they really aren't that fast. Their more likely speed is about 20 mph.

Many times, dolphins and sharks will live and feed together peacefully. Some of the bite scars seen on dolphins may be because they were feeding with a shark who went into a frenzy and bit the dolphin without meaning to.

Sharks have no bones, just soft cartilage. Their inner organs are easily hurt by ramming. In these battles, when the dolphins ram the sharks, the dolphins usually win and drive the sharks away.

When a shark attacks a dolphin who is in a group, the other dolphins surround the shark and start ramming its stomach with their snouts.

DOLPHINS AND SHARKS   23

In the early days of sea parks, dolphins and sharks often shared the same tank peacefully. But enough fights started, so this is no longer done.

When they fight, a shark is a dolphin's scariest enemy. Some sharks like to eat dolphins. But sharks usually only attack young dolphins, or older, weaker, or helpless dolphins.

Because shark skin is so rough—just like sandpaper—dolphins don't actually like to ram sharks. The shark's rough skin painfully scrapes the dolphin's tender skin. Dolphins rarely start fights with sharks unless they are attacked first.

Flipper says:
I understand that sharks sometimes want to eat dolphins. After all, everyone gets hungry. But that hammerhead shark, Scar, ought to try eating mullet. They're easy to catch 'cause they're kind of stupid, and they taste great! I bet Scar wished he'd tried mullet instead of Sandy after I rammed him!

Flipper says:

Didn't I help find the barrels? Didn't I tap the ball just right to let Porter know where they were? Didn't I teach Sandy how to use a snorkel? (Well, almost). Didn't I keep coming back, no matter what? Didn't I . . . Well, you get the idea. I really *do* love you humans!

Dolphins and humans have been together for over 3,000 years. They have helped one another at times, and they have even played together. An ancient wall painting found in a palace on the island of Crete shows swimming dolphins.

2,500 years ago the ancient Greek philosopher Aristotle wrote about dolphins talking to people. He noticed that dolphins sounded just like humans. They could even say vowels and consonants; however, Aristotle noted, they have trouble putting them together!

At some Australian beaches, dolphins will swim right into shore because they love to play with the swimmers—especially children!

The seafaring ancient Greeks had a favorite theme showing a boy riding a dolphin. They put this on many of their coins and their pottery, too.

In Brazil, dolphins even help people catch fish. When a school of fish comes by, the dolphins splash to let the fishermen know it's time to cast their nets. The dolphins then eat the fish which don't get caught in the net.

Recently discovered South African cave drawings show images of dolphins; and at least one image shows a man swimming with them!

In ancient myths, dolphins were often good luck and known for being friendly to humans. They always appeared in the role of helping people.

Even in modern times, dolphins are still helping people. They will often push people to shore if they are adrift. During World War II, two dolphins pushed a raft of downed American airmen all the way to land.

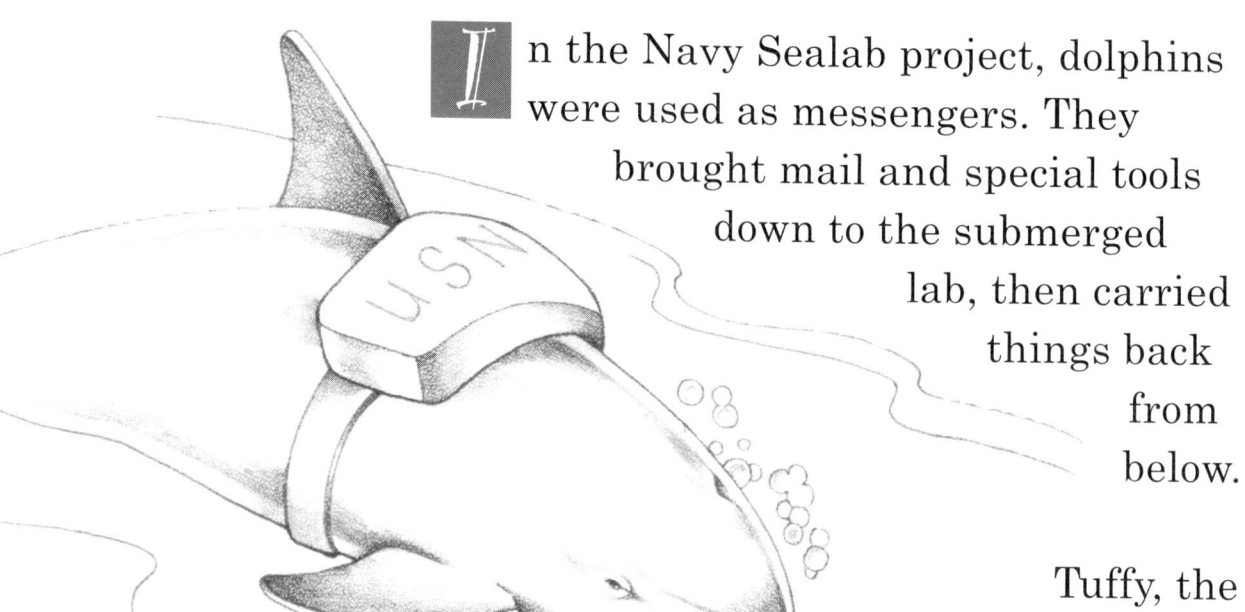

In the Navy Sealab project, dolphins were used as messengers. They brought mail and special tools down to the submerged lab, then carried things back from below.

Tuffy, the deep-diving dolphin at Sealab, would bring down his own packaged fish reward, and receive it on the ocean floor from one of the aquanauts. Since the Sealab dolphins were free-swimming, scientists weren't sure if they would return to the Sealab once they left. So the dolphins were trained to answer a sonic signal—and they never failed to come back when called!

Flipper says:
Dolphins have always been helpful! Who needs training? We're already smart! Like, did I bring tools and rope and stuff down to Sandy from Kim on the boat, or what? Did I carry the camera that Marvin built, or what? We're just natural helpers!

Dolphins often accompany human Navy divers as their diving buddies. A dolphin's senses are much better at picking up any underwater dangers, such as sharks. They are also able to cover a much larger area because they can swim so fast. Dolphins can be trained to patrol beaches and swimming areas for sharks and other predators that can harm humans.

Sometimes search and rescue boats have a hard time finding floating survivors of airplane or boat accidents. Scientists are working on sonic signal devices which will attract specially trained rescue dolphins. With sonar, the dolphins will help find the humans!

Dolphins have been used to find missing pieces of oceanographic equipment. They simply follow the sound of a sonic signaling device attached to the equipment!

Dangers in the Dolphin Environment

The two sea creatures that feed on dolphins are sharks and killer whales. Killer whales will sometimes trap dolphins in a circle the same way dolphins trap the schools of fish they feed on.

Even though the ocean is a dangerous place to live, the greatest enemy dolphins face are the dangers created by people. Tuna swim in large schools, and they like to swim under dolphin pods. When commercial fishermen move schools of tuna with huge nets, the dolphins can get caught as well.

Tuna nets are called *purse-seins*. Once fish swim into the net, the bottom is closed and the fish are trapped inside. Unable to surface for air, any trapped dolphins will drown.

Other kinds of fishing nets are also dangerous for dolphins. Drift nets sometimes get wrapped around a dolphin's flippers, holding the animal down until it drowns. Drift nets are deadly to seals and whales as well.

Most nations, including our own, dump garbage and toxic waste into the ocean. A whole population of European harbor dolphins has been destroyed by these poisons.

The oceans around the world are getting so dirty that if Beluga whales wash up on shore nowadays, they are classified as toxic waste. That's because Beluga whales eat fish that are bottom feeders. The bottom of the ocean is where all the waste settles after it has been dumped. Dolphins often eat bottom fish, too.

Many people are interested in protecting dolphins. Some tuna companies have stopped using purse-seins. Their cans of tuna are marked "Dolphin Safe." Buying only dolphin safe tuna is a way to support the protection of dolphins.

Flipper says:
Trust me! If you have a choice between Dirk Moran and a shark, take the shark! Dirk Moran was dumping Dioxin, a deadly poison, into the water. Dioxin was in the fish, and I ate some of those fish. And I sure did get sick! Hey! Don't you humans eat those fish, too? You better be careful what goes into our oceans and rivers!

The freshwater dolphins of India and China are almost extinct. There is so much pollution in the rivers where they live, the few that remain are getting sick and dying.

Protecting Dolphins

Flipper says:
You see now that Dirk Moran was doing two bad things. He shot at us dolphins, and for that alone he should be punished! And he was also dumping toxic waste. That man definitely belongs in jail!

The United Nations World Charter for Nature recently said, "All areas of the earth, both land and sea, shall be subject to special principles of conservation." The trouble is, not everyone is obeying these laws that their country's leaders agreed to obey.

There are now strong laws protecting dolphins from being hunted for food, leather, or oil. There are also laws protecting them from capture, and from fishermen who think it's OK to hurt dolphins.

Pollution is still a problem, however. In 1972, 26 nations signed The Stockholm Declaration on the Human Environment.

It said that dumping "toxic substances . . . must be halted in order to ensure that irreversible damage is not inflicted on the ecosystems."

In 1982, 105 nations signed The Nairobi Declaration that said, ". . . pollution of the seas and careless use and disposal of hazardous substances constitute grave threats."

Both of these declarations are intended to protect sea life and the marine environment.

Caring for Stranded Dolphins

Sometimes dolphins beach themselves and get stranded. This is usually because they are sick or hurt. Sometimes their internal sonar compasses have been hurt or they've been scared by sharks.

Usually, only one animal is stranded, but sometimes there are mass strandings—anywhere from 3 to 100 dolphins are beached and dying. Some scientists think this happens because an honored member of the pod is very sick, and the others are keeping it company during its last hours.

Flipper says: Lucky for me, Cathy knew just what to do when I was so sick and hurt. Study these rules! You never know when I might need your help!

If you see a stranded dolphin:

What to do:

- Keep the dolphin cool and wet. They have no sweat glands and will literally burn up from the inside.

- If possible, move the dolphin into shallow water. Its own weight can hurt its inner organs. Hold its blowhole above water so it can breathe.

- Always keep water out of a dolphin's blowhole, otherwise it will drown.

- If you can't get much water to the dolphin, coat every exposed part—except the blowhole and eyes—with a mixture of hydrous lanolin and petroleum jelly. This keeps its skin from heating up and blistering.

- If you can't move the dolphin, keep it wet. If it's on its side, roll it so the blowhole is up. Cover its eyes with a wet cloth or paper towel so they won't be harmed by the sun.

- Call the nearest sea park, museum, marine laboratory, or animal rescue organization for help. They are usually listed in the local telephone book. The scientists who work there will travel any distance necessary to save a stranded sea animal.

- If the dolphin is already dead, call anyway. Scientists need to know why the animal died. They will want to study the carcass.

Flipper says:
You see, I really got to love Sandy, Porter, Kim, and even Pete the Pelican. Sandy gave me snacks, and I rewarded him with tricks. Humans are very intelligent for land animals. And they're a cinch to train! So even when Buck took me out to the open sea, I decided to come back—'cause friends are forever!

Captive dolphins are no longer "wild animals," and they don't always want to be returned to the wild. Sometimes released dolphins will purposely chase animal collecting boats just so they can be recaptured!

Note From the Editors:

Now that you know so much about these wonderful mammals that share our oceans, you should think about the message dolphins are trying to send us here on land: We owe it to ourselves, our children, and all future children to protect the environment. After all, we share this planet with all living things—not just other people. Taking care of all the creatures is the same as taking care of ourselves. Write letters to your local congresspersons and the President of the United States. Ask them to help you protect your world, yourself, and your new friends— the dolphins!

THE END

Some dolphins who have lived in captivity for a long time refuse to eat live fish. They've gotten used to dinners that don't wiggle—and some even prefer them!

Newly captured dolphins often become so well adapted, in a few weeks they prefer human company to that of other dolphins. Some will only perform for their own trainer and ignore everyone else.

Sometimes, sea park dolphins and whales teach each other the tricks they learn without ever having been trained by a person. One whale taught herself all the dolphin tricks by hauling herself up on the edge of her tank and watching. Once she got so far up, she actually fell out of the tank!

Don't you agree that animals this smart and friendly deserve our care and protection?